HALF PINT EDITIONS

Just Goldens

PHOTOGRAPHS BY DALE C. SPARTAS
TEXT BY TOM DAVIS

WILLOW CREEK PRESS
Minocqua, Wisconsin

Design and production by Heather M. McElwain.

Published by WILLOW CREEK PRESS, INC.
PO Box 147, Minocqua, WI 54548

For more information on Willow Creek Press titles,
call 1-800-850-9453.

Individual poster prints of the photographs in this book are
available for purchase directly from the photographer.
Write to: Dale C. Spartas, P.O. Box 1367,
Bozeman, MT 59715, or call (406) 585-2244.

Library of Congress Cataloging-in-Publication Data
Spartas, Dale C.
     Just goldens / photographs by Dale C. Spartas ; text by
Tom Davis. -- Half pint ed.
          p.   cm. (Half pint series)
     ISBN 1-57223-218-8
     1. Golden retriever.   2. Golden retriever--Pictorial
works.   3. Photography of dogs.   I. Davis, Tom.   II.
Title.   III. Series.
SF429.G63S63   1999
636.752'7--dc21   98-52366
                                                CIP

Printed in Canada.

Contents

Dedication

I dedicate this book to my four wonderful children,
Kaitlin, Elizabeth, Sarah and Christo,
whose innocence, beauty, idealism and love
have added immeasurably to life's quality.

– D.C.S.

Acknowledgements

I'd like to acknowledge the following people for their time, patience, support and beautiful goldens. Bill Baldus & Buck, Bev Bellehuemer & Dusty, Amy Branson & Honey, The Brewster Family, Tom Butler & April, Ken Conger & Libby, Byron Dugree & Reb, Chuck Forest Craig Janssen, Ed Gerrity and Flying Falcon Kennels, Gwen & Lakota, Bob Goodwillie & Rusty, Roper Green & Grizz, Jeff Herbert & Tanker, Joe Kerchinski & Gunner, M.B. Kolarchek, Ken Nielsen & Brody, Donna Pace, Amy & Autumn Peterson & Bow, Jennifer Petrusha & Buster, Ken Raynor, Jack Risselman & Snickers, Dale Sexton, Gary Smith & Addie, Tom and Pat Stonehouse & Casey, Rick Wollum & Ranier, and everyone else who has helped with this project.

PORTRAITS

*Aristocrats –
With the Common Touch*

The old dog knows; the young dogs want to. Natural inquisitiveness and intelligence are where the journey to wisdom begins, but only the long road of experience can put that soulful, knowing look in a golden's eyes.

as anyone ever met a golden retriever they didn't like? Or walked past one on the street without stopping to scratch a silky ear, the dog leaning into the pressure of your touch, its eyes half-closed in bliss? If ever a breed was affectionate to a fault, it's the golden. They're people dogs, pure and simple, and if you own one there's never any doubt that you're the center of its universe. Chances are, too, that it will become the center of yours. Golden owners and their dogs didn't invent the mutual admiration society – they perfected it.

LIVING WITH GOLDENS

*Darlings, Rogues
and Rascals*

N o book about dogs
would be complete
without some doggerel,
so here goes:

It flies through the air
With the greatest of ease:
The golden retriever
Trained to chase down Frisbees.

The golden's even temperament and happy-go-lucky personality mask a desire to retrieve that, when the match is struck, burns with white-hot intensity.

Goldens aren't particular about *what* they retrieve. A training dummy is fine – but so is a ball, a stick, a ripe, dead carp, or Dad's favorite pair of slippers. And if there's a chance to mix in a quick game of keep-away, so much the better.

Professional trainers – which is to say, people in a position to know – will tell you that goldens tend to be "thinkers" as opposed to "doers." In other words, they like to mull things over and consider their options before choosing an appropriate course of action. This independence of mind occasionally puts them at loggerheads with their human partners. (One of the most legendary "incidents" in field trial history occurred when a champion golden and its handler had a difference of opinion regarding the proper sequence in which to accomplish a test that required multiple retrieves.) It also explains why you don't really *command* a golden. First, you define your terms; then, you coax, cajole and cross your fingers. Any way you cut it, though, possession is still nine-tenths of the law.

O f course, some retrieves are more problematic than
others. The job usually gets done – but the integrity of
the retrieved object can't always be guaranteed.

You can't play as hard as golden retrievers do without indulging in regular siestas. They don't need much provocation, either. A little exercise, a warm patch of sunshine, and it's snooze city, baby. Generations of goldens have refined napping into an art form.

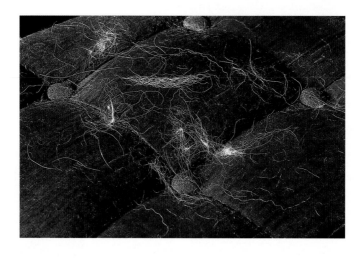

B eauty, as they say, has its price. The golden's luxurious coat requires serious upkeep: shampooing, combing, brushing, de-burring. Still, most goldens – and their owners – seem to enjoy these rituals of vanity. And if fussy friends comment about the dog hair that finds its way onto (and into) everything in sight, maybe it's time to get new friends.

Whenever possible, goldens prefer being with people – specifically, with *their* people. They chafe at being confined or, even worse, left behind, and on the occasions when they're instructed to stay put, you can almost see the smoke coming out of their ears. ("Leave *me* in the car, after all we've been through together? Why, you ungrateful !@#$%! I'll fix *your* wagon.") No one ever said that goldens couldn't be willful – or, for that matter, downright hard-headed. Funny thing is, it makes you love them all the more.

Goldens can be frustrating, irritating, even exasperating. But all it takes is a certain look – a cock of the ear, a furrow in the brow – to smooth things over, put the smile back on your face, and fill your heart with joy. No one stays mad at a golden retriever for very long.

I n every life, a little rain must fall. A golden retriever is an umbrella with soul, a friend you can count on no matter how tough the going gets. Lost your job? The love of your life ran off with your neighbor? Your golden's there for you, pilgrim.

Goldens are poor choices for people uncomfortable with public displays of affection. It wouldn't be far wrong to call them brazen. Big, wet, sloppy kisses are their stock-in-trade, and while you grimace when you receive one, it's really just to conceal your delight.

S ome dogs are content with an occasional pat on the head and a briefly expressed term of endearment. Not goldens – they demand the maximum dosage. They bask in attention, wallow in it, soak it up like a sponge. Fair's fair, after all: You can't expect them to dish out those heaping portions of the sweet stuff unless they're enjoying a steady diet of it themselves.

The dress code for walking goldens can be summed up in one word: casual. As good as they make you look (and feel), you could throw on the rattiest clothes in your dresser and anyone who saw you would swear you'd stepped right out of a Ralph Lauren ad. This fact has not been lost on Madison Avenue.

Like celestial bodies, golden retrievers exert a kind of gravitational attraction. It's a virtual law of nature that a solitary golden will soon have company, pulling passersby into its orbit.

G oldens don't have to be told that they're just a little better than other dogs; they know. They're not above gently lording their superiority over the less fortunate members of canine society, either.

For decades, it was believed that the golden retriever was descended from mysterious "Russian circus dogs" that Lord Tweedmouth,

the acknowledged father of the breed, purchased circa 1860. Only in 1952, when Tweedmouth's detailed records were discovered, was this account

revealed to be a complete hoax, perpetrated by unknown pranksters who, to quote the late Richard Wolters, "must have giggled all the way to their graves." Still, there's no denying that goldens are born show-offs. They're shameless hams, and they relish an audience. It almost

makes you wonder if one of those Russian circus dogs didn't manage to scale the fence at Lord Tweedmouth's kennel.

As far as the average golden retriever is concerned, its status as a member of the "sporting" category is inclusive of *all* outdoor pursuits, not just hunting. It must be admitted, however, that its role as a fishing

dog is largely supervisory. And part of being a good supervisor is knowing when to stick your nose in, and when to butt out, close the office door, and tell the secretary to hold your calls.

SPORTING COMPANIONS

*The Ancient
Partnership
Endures*

G etting there is half the fun – especially when your destination is a hidden, jewel-like pond that only you, and your golden, know about. It's one of the little secrets you share, part of the private territory of your sporting partnership. The two of you could find your way there in the dark, and often do, crunching through the snow in the bitter, pre-dawn chill, your breath like a hovering ghost. Nothing need be said; you're occupying old, familiar roles, and you're connected by the bright filament of a primal calling.

The easy-going attitude displayed around the house vanishes once the hunt is on. This is serious business, fraught with such critical decisions as the proper placement of the decoys. And, because you're partners in this, you can almost hear your golden putting in his two cents' worth: "A little more to the right . . . a little more . . . too far . . . perfect." It's almost as if an interior decorating gene snuck in there somewhere.

Everything that the golden is begins with this: the irresistible desire to retrieve, to find downed game and *bring it back*. It's a miracle, really, an irrevocably encoded behavior that, taken out of context, seems like an amusing parlor trick. But to a waterfowl hunter, it's the *sine qua non*, the olive in the martini, the distilled and potent essence of the sport.

When gunner and golden have each done their part, an honest pride wells up – a pride that is palpable and satisfying as a drake mallard in the hand.

G oldens are true all-purpose gundogs. Their tastes are catholic; if it has feathers, they'll hunt it and pick it up. Those who gun over goldens are rarely in a hurry for the bird to be delivered to hand. They'd just as soon let their dog strike a pose and hold it for a while, so they can savor the moment and admire the auxtaposition of beauty.

A t some point in the dim and distant past, man quit kidding himself and concluded that, as predators go, he left a lot to be desired. He was slow; he was clumsy; his senses were dull. To his credit, though, he had brains enough to recruit the dog as his ally. It was one of the shrewdest moves *homo sapiens* ever made. The dog became his eyes, ears and, particularly, his nose; a tougher, faster, more courageous extension of himself. This alliance was thousands of years old by the time the golden entered the picture – but there are those who would argue that it's never been closer to perfection. They're the people who hunt with golden retrievers.

Oh, the boundless energy of youth! The muscles like coiled springs of tempered steel, the enthusiasm as hot and bright as the blue flame from a welder's torch. Young dogs can ride this wave of adrenaline from dawn 'til dusk, never tiring (hell, never drawing a deep breath!), letting nothing stand in their purposeful way. Whatever they lack in technique, they make up for in sheer drive, in ferocious determination. And when you're feeling bone-weary yourself, they pull you along in the slipstream.

Muddy Waters used to sing (as only Muddy could) about how young horses are fast, but old horses know what's going on. It's the same with old goldens: There's no wasted motion, no frivolity, just a job to be done, and a hard-edged, professional way of doing it. Wisdom is the compensation for the erosion of the body. Of course, a poignant aura surrounds any hunt with a grizzled, gray-muzzled veteran, a dog with whom you share a history, a dog that has taught you things – about birds, about living, about yourself – that you never understood before. But that's between the two of you, as private and personal as the contents of a diary.

PUPPIES!

Simply Irresistible

PUPPIES!

Simply Irresistible

Whoever coined the term "warm fuzzies" to describe a feeling of complete contentment must have had golden retriever puppies in mind. They're simply irresistible, and they have a smell — musky, damp, sweet-sour — like nothing else on earth.

There is no such thing as window-shopping for a golden retriever puppy. You may have the best intentions of "just looking" when you go to check out a litter, but the fact of the matter is that as soon as you lay eyes on those frolicking, floppy-eared bundles of yellow fur, your goose is cooked. One of the puppies will meet your gaze with a smile that reaches all the way to your heart, a smile that says "I'm the one. Take *me* home." And you will. You irrevocably, joyfully, and certainly will.

P hysics teachers devote hours of class time to explaining the concepts of potential energy and kinetic energy, as well as the relationship between the two. A field trip to visit a litter of goldens would achieve the same result – and be a heck of a lot more fun. Plus, you'd have to memorize just two equations: Potential energy = Golden puppies in a pen; Kinetic energy = Golden puppies on the loose. There would also be a natural tie-in to the law stating that bodies in motion tend to stay in motion.

The capacity of puppies to engage in mock combat seems limitless. Suddenly, one gets that mischievous gleam in its eye and pounces on the nearest available littermate, its jaws clamping down on whatever tender body part gets in the way. These contests are surprisingly fierce: The fur flies, the teeth flash like drawn knives, and big, menacing growls emerge from those little, adorable throats. They wrestle, roll one over the other, disengage, shake, and come back for more. A clear-cut victor can rarely be identified, and if pride is wounded, there's always a rematch to look forward to.

Puppies and mud go together like Astaire and Rogers, bourbon and branch, leather and lace. This goes a long way toward explaining why puppies and carpets are usually a bad mix.

S uch declarations are always subject to debate, but a strong case can be made that the golden retriever has brought more happiness to more children than any other breed.

Goldens are the original chow-hounds. If you're packing anything edible, you can run – but you can't hide. They'll sniff you out, surround you, and make you surrender the goods. Your picture might as well be on display at the post office.

A t last, there comes a day when the pup's mettle must be tested. You can't wait any longer; you have to find out if the raw material, the right stuff, is there. You're on pins and needles as you lob the training dummy, hoping, wondering . . . And the pup – awkward, uncoordinated, but intensely focused – gallops out, grabs the dummy as best it can, and proudly brings it back. Once again, the legacy of blood, of breeding, has been proven. Was there really any doubt?

Needless to say, you don't truly *train* a puppy to retrieve. It comes naturally; the desire is hard-wired into their genetic circuitry. Your role is to refine and perfect this desire, using such tools as repetition, association, and praise. It helps to have an eager pupil, too, and a well-bred golden puppy will hang on your every word.

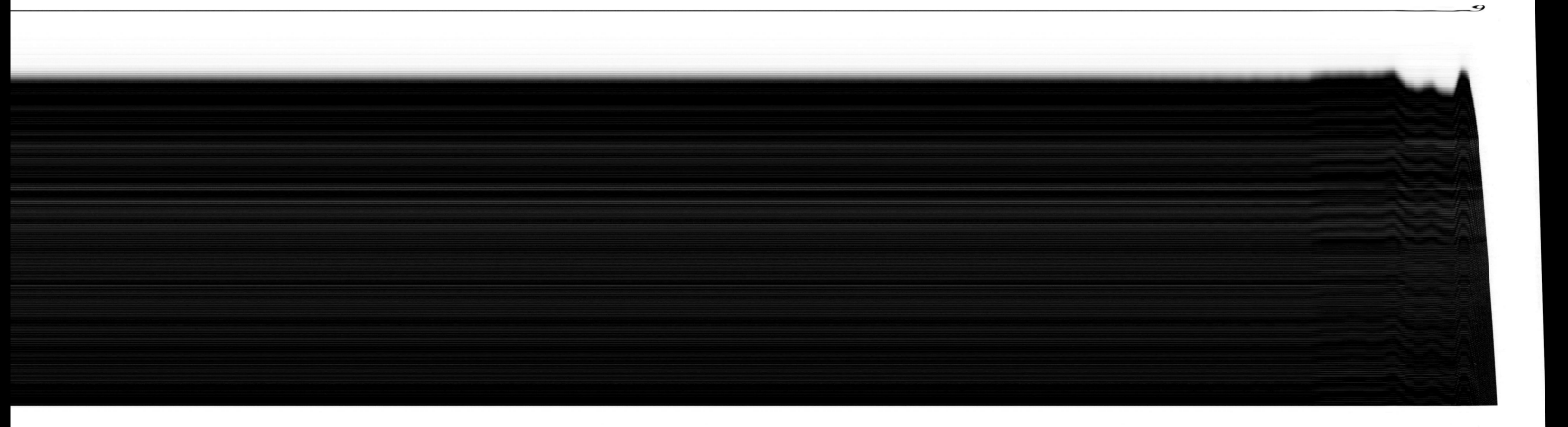

Nothing is safe from a puppy's teeth. They're stiletto sharp – like tiny ivory daggers – and every opportunity to employ them is seized. Shoelaces, pants cuffs, and other floppy, dangly, eye-level items make tempting targets, but everything is ultimately fair game. Wherever a puppy looks, it sees a sign that reads, *Chew Here.*

W hat is a golden retriever puppy? The stuff that dreams are made of – the sweetest dreams of all.